Fight On!
Fighting lessons to help find God's best in the midst of a trial

Christin Loera

Published by Caring Resources

ALL RIGHTS RESERVED

Scripture quotations from the NEW KING JAMES VERSION.
Copyright © 1982 by Thomas Nelson: Nashville

Copyright © 2020 Christin Loera
Caring Resources
818 Shadowstone Place.
Nashville, TN 37220
USA
www.caringresources.com
wecare@caringresources.com

Written Permission must be secured from Christin Loera and Caring Resources to reproduce any part of this book in any manner whatsoever. ALL RIGHTS RESERVED.

CONTENTS

Fighting Lessons	1
Fighting Lesson #1 Rest	7
Fighting Lesson #2 Choose to Meditate on the Right Thing	15
Fighting Lesson #3 Don't Be Passive. Don't Be Paralyzed	23
Fighting Lesson #4 Trust	31
Fighting Lesson #5 Love Correction	43
Fighting Lesson #6 Stay Present	51
Fighting Lesson #7 Become Undignified	59
Fighting Lesson #8 Delay is Not Defeat (In fact, delay is not even delay.)	67
Fighting Lesson #9 Our Most Powerful Weapon: The Word of God	75
Fighting Lesson #10 Humility, Humility, Humility . . . It Wasn't Me!	83
Fight On Conclusion	91

Fighting Lessons

Trials. James 1:2 says to "count it all joy when you fall into various trials." When we hear the word *trials*, it often provokes an emotion of anxiety and nervousness, knowing there is only one of two outcomes: success or failure. Of course, it is not in our nature to want to endure a trial. Even more, it is not our instinct to be joyful at the thought of a trial, much less be joyful in it. In my flesh, if I could go to sleep, then wake up, and a trial be over, that would be fine with me. As we know, our flesh is often (really 100%) in opposition to what the Lord wants to do in us and through us. In God's kingdom, a trial is not about success and failure, but rather it's about an opportunity to grow, to transform, and to be blessed. We are often in a situation that allows God to prove Himself to be who He says He is—if we let Him. So, to avoid a trial does not help our development as a child of God. In fact, avoidance of trials can lull us into a place of dullness, lethargy, and compromise. That is not what I want! I want to be all that God has made me to be and called me to be—to be a vessel for His kingdom, His glory.

Each trial is different for each person. Our history, our experiences, our mindset, our spiritual maturity, our circumstances all set the stage—each unique—each with purpose—for each trial we face. Similarly, victory is different for each person. Victory is not always defined as the trial ending with favorable circumstances for us: a win. For some, victory is becoming able to face conflict with overwhelming peace and steadfastness of joy. For others, victory is growth in spiritual maturity and wisdom, seeing things from God's perspective. Victory is the eternal fruit that is produced, and the eternal rewards that are secured. Of course, we know our ultimate victory is our eternal life with Jesus, with no sorrow, no evil, no tears, and no trials! But it is important to keep this perspective in mind, or else we might lose sight of the victory we gain.

For me, this trial has deep-rooted heart desires at stake. You see, since I was a young girl, I always thought adoption was an amazing thing. I wanted to adopt children—it was already established in my heart. This was further solidified when my mother, in an effort to teach me the beauty of childbirth, took my sister and me (I was twelve years old at the time), to see a baby being born. Instead of immense joy, I was in immense shock and horror. From that moment on, there was no question that adoption was for me!

Moving forward twenty-four years in 2009, I married my husband, Ernie. Since I was a little older, we knew we needed to work on the "kid thing" right away. Within our first eighteen months of marriage, we found out we could not have biological children. While this diagnosis would be devastating to many, I was okay with it, as I still wanted to adopt children. Thankfully, Ernie's heart quickly softened to the idea of adoption. By the end of 2010, we had filled out our application for a domestic adoption.

In February 2011, we received a call that a young lady from Southern California wanted us to parent her child, who was to be born in March. Ernie and I quickly flew out to California (with my mother, of course) and established a relationship with this young lady. We took her to the doctor, and I was able to see the sonogram of this beautiful baby boy. Within two weeks, she was in labor. I was actually in the delivery room and saw the baby born (and was not horrified). Ernie and I took him back to the nursery and watched him get cleaned up. We held him. We changed him. We rocked him. We kissed him. We loved him. He was beautiful. We left the hospital that night not knowing that we would never see that beautiful boy again. The young lady changed her mind and decided to raise him. It was her right to do so, but it made it no less painful for us.

Weeks went by, then months. There were calls from the agency to check in on us, but I knew from the information we had been given from them that in the worldly view, hope was fading. But, we stayed in faith for our children. The Lord even gave me a beautiful new perspective on the entire process. We were not to be praying for our children to come, but we should be praying for the children to come who we were supposed to parent. I know that can seem like semantics to many, but I knew the difference in my heart, and it gave me hope.

At the end of January 2012, we received a call regarding two boys who might need a home. The agency was unsure if this would even be an option, but they wanted us to pray about it, since it wouldn't be a baby. The two boys were fifteen months and two years old. We prayed, and we knew this was from the Lord. And then . . .

In February 2012, my husband and I were able to meet our two children for the very first time. They were beautiful. They were innocent. The oldest could walk and talk; the youngest just sat and ate. At that moment, my husband and I were so excited to take them home and embark on a journey to make them a permanent part of our family. We spent countless hours talking about what they should eat (I mean, we have to be the "healthy" parents, right?), contemplating what they should play (because they need to be educated while they play), where we needed to take them—or not take them (heaven forbid we introduce them to something too soon). Yes, we were first time parents, treating both like first born children. We were so careful, so cautious.

A year went by, and the adoption process moved slowly along. Yes, there was a little frustration, but we knew we had a word from the Lord that these were our children. And, then it happened. July 2013, a year and a half after these children came to live with us, we received news that the adoption of our children was to be contested. WHAT?!? I mean, we had a word from the Lord. We had support on every side. The boys had been with us for a year and a half. This truly came out of left field, and I believe it was the intent of the enemy to use this to try and knock us off our foundation, our sure footing in Jesus.

After prayer and discussion with our community, Ernie and I knew in our hearts that this was our trial. We had no doubt of who our God was (and is). We had no doubt of what He could do (and does). And, we also knew we had words from the Lord to stand on. The question was, how were we going to CHOOSE to walk through this? Since I knew I had an opportunity to grow as we walked through this, I made a specific request from the Lord. I asked that God would teach me how to be an effective, tough fighter in this trial, for me and for others. That was how I was choosing to walk through it, and God answered.

This book lays out the lessons I learned. I did learn how to fight. And, I learned that I am loved by an awesome Father! I want you to learn the same. I know not all trials come in the same shapes and sizes, circumstances or degrees, but I do believe these are lessons that can be used in any trial that comes your way.

At the beginning of this trial, I heard the Lord say loud and clear the following, and it has been a word I return to often:

> *You will have victory.*
> *My arm is not too short.*
> *My hand has not grown weak.*
> *My voice is not silent.*
> *I am Almighty God.*

He is a big God, after all!

Fighting Lesson #1

Rest

Rest is not what one thinks of when starting a fight. I'm sure Muhammad Ali, or any other famous boxer for that matter, did not prepare for a fight with a nap. I maybe could see them shadow boxing, jumping around, moving, getting their blood flowing and their muscles loose. Now, I am no boxer, but I am a woman of action. When it is time to get something done, I want to go ahead and move! I am more on the "Ready-Fire-Aim" end of the spectrum, so this lesson seemed counter-intuitive to me.

Oh, but God's knowledge and wisdom are so different than that of the world! I knew my lessons had begun when I heard the Lord speak September 26, 2013:

> *When did you come to see Me as a slave driver? That is not what I am.*
>
> *I will teach you how to fight. You have to understand that being a good fighter means you know when to rest –when to wait on Me, patiently, for renewed strength. I do not expect you to have supernatural sustaining power indefinitely, or else you would not come to Me and see your need for Me. I know your frailties. I know your weakness. Wait patiently for*

Me, and I will renew your strength. Then you can fight effectively.

Well, He knew AND knows me. He knew my fleshly tendencies. He knew my faulty thinking. And, He knew that if I didn't get this lesson, the trial would be long, exhausting, miserable, and fruitless for my spirit man and for my physical state.

Why was this Lesson #1 for me?

- I had a wrong perception of God. I did see Him as a slave driver. It is my nature to perform. I believed if I performed long enough, hard enough, and good enough, then God would do what I wanted. I could simply impress Him into action with my endurance, with my work ethic, with my unending acts.

- My fleshly nature is to be a people pleaser. If I am having to wait on God to do something and I don't see Him act fast enough (in my time), I feel that I need to perform for Him to move His heart towards me . . . so He will act right then! This is a lie that I believed for most of my life: if I could just please God, He would do what I wanted Him to do. At the core of it is a spirit of manipulation and impatience, and that was my MO (modus operandi) for a long time. I would try to manipulate God to move on my behalf when I thought He needed to move.

- I am human. As much as I hate to admit it sometimes, I do wear out. I do get tired. I need rest. When I am tired, I don't take any news well. When I am tired, I overreact and have trouble keeping thoughts captive. I can become mentally exhausted just trying to remember that God is bigger than my circumstance. It is easy to become ensnared in the lies of the enemy, because when I am tired, it is so much easier to just accept them rather than fight them.

Yes, the ugly truth was right there in the first line of Lesson #1. He was telling me that my perception of Him was wrong, that my way of "spiritual" operations was based in manipulation and impatience, and that I was weak . . . and all with the word REST. This is not something I wanted to hear right off the bat, but it was needed. If I did not get a right perspective of God and truly trust in Him, there was no reason to move forward in the lessons.

So to REST is a lesson that helps strengthen on three fronts:

Spiritually: Matthew 11:28-30 says:
Come to Me, all you who labor and are heavy laden, and I will give you rest. Take My yoke upon you and learn from Me, for I am gentle and lowly in heart, and you will find rest for your souls. For My yoke is easy and My burden is light.

Spiritual rest means we are not working in our own strength or in our own sufficiency, but truly relying on Him for strength and on Him to be our sufficiency. It means we take the pressure off ourselves to *perform*, and we put the pressure on the One who has already won. Jesus invited us to give Him our burdens, to yoke up with Him, and learn how to walk through every laborious and heavy situation by watching Him. We take our cues from Him. The promise is that as we yoke up to Him, we find rest for our souls.

This is tough for many of us to swallow, as we all want to be perceived as strong and steady. The truth is, we are truly strong and steady if we are letting Jesus be our strong and our steady. In my own person, in my own spirit man, I am not an immovable object. But I do know the One who is immovable, and if I lean into Him, if I yoke up to Him, if I bind myself to Him, then I become immovable.

Mentally: Proverbs 24:4-5 says:
A wise warrior is better than a strong one, and a man of knowledge than one of strength; for you should wage war with sound guidance—victory comes with many counselors.

There is a level of exhaustion that comes when we try to figure things out in our own mental capacity. It is in our human nature to want to know "why?" We can spend countless hours trying to come up with answers of why things are happening, what we need to do, and how we need to do it. We also know how exhausting it is when we spend so much mental energy on questions such as these. Thankfully, this is not what the Lord requires of us, nor expects from us.

We are admonished to walk in the Lord's wisdom throughout Scriptures. But in so many instances where it speaks of wisdom, it also tells us that we are to ask the Lord for it, and as it says in James 1:5, He will provide it liberally. The Lord wants us to seek His wisdom, and then use it! As believers, we are given the mind of Christ, which is omniscient—meaning He knows all. When we rest in His wisdom, and trust in His strategy, we will not wear out mentally. We will not be set up for days of anxiety or a nervous breakdown. We can remain sharp, we will remain in peace, we will remain sane, and we will be victorious despite the circumstances.

Physically: Isaiah 40:28-31 says:

Have you not known? Have you not heard? The everlasting God, the Lord, the Creator of the ends of the earth, neither faints nor is weary. His understanding is unsearchable. He gives power to the weak, and to those who have no might He increases strength. Even the youths shall faint and be weary, and the young men shall utterly fall, but those who wait on the Lord shall renew their strength; they shall mount up with wings like eagles, they shall run and not be weary, they shall walk and not faint.

I love that the Lord says "and to those who have no might He increased strength." He knows what we need for the battle, for the fight. He knows that our bodies are not meant for unending pursuit of the enemy, for ceaseless activity, for constant movement. Our physical bodies need rest. And, the

Lord's answer for that? To wait on Him to renew our strength. To be patient. To be obedient to His word. To not put ourselves in the place of God, thinking (or acting as if) we have super-human strength, that we see all and know all.

As we rest physically, our minds can rest, too. We can gain the perspective we need. We can be encouraged in the Word of God. We can give our bodies time to heal and be refreshed, so as we go out for the next "round," we are in top condition, top form, and can walk victorious. Let us rest, and be in anticipation of what God will do.

Anticipation

Questions answered, but answers yet fulfilled,
I say, "Praise be to the Lord Most High."
Promises made but not yet seen,
I say, "Praise be to the Lord. Lover of my soul!"
What my hope is, and its source is One in the Same.
Wrapped in the I AM.
Tangled, twisted, and entwined with El Elyon.
Seated in the heavenliness and right by my side,
Directing the forces of nature,
Brushing my hair from my ear,
Whispering
"Watch what I am about to do."

Christin Moore (Loera) (March 2, 2007)

Reflection:

- Where, or on whom, are you relying for your strength?

- Are there places where you are not resting? Why?

- Where are those places where you are putting yourself as equal to God, trying to do everything all the time?

- What does rest in the Lord look like for your life?

- What is the strategy the Lord is speaking to you in order to find spiritual, mental, and physical rest?

Fighting Lesson #2

Choose to Meditate on the Right Thing

The second lesson came rather quickly after the first. In our trial preparation, my husband and I had to do a variety of things, such as get fingerprinted (again), have phone interviews, and fill out more paperwork. We had been diligent to do all that was asked, yet it still seemed as if there was always another thing for us to do—another hoop for us to jump through. And, things did not always go so smoothly. At this point (the end of September), we had our trial postponed twice, and we had some of our information returned in the mail, marked with an error. On October 1, 2013, my journal entry read:

Yesterday was a lesson in fighting. After finding mail with our returned fingerprints, I was angry and sad, thinking "not another attack." Then, I went to bed. (Reference Lesson #1) In reading the Word the next morning, I was distracted. But, knowing I needed to get in faith, I began to meditate on the Word and who God is. In the car as I was praying, I felt I was at a crossroads. I could choose to 1) get in fear and doubt God, OR 2) think about the Lionel Richie concert, OR 3) believe the Word—remember all He has done for me, how I have seen Him work, and believe and declare who He is. I chose the last option, and with that, fretting was gone. With that, I had complete peace.

(Know that I don't randomly think about Lionel Richie. Just a few days before we were invited to have a pre-concert dinner with him and fifty of his friends. We then attended his concert, and were seated in floor seats close to the stage, which was great.) This was a "when the rubber meets the road" type of experience. I had to choose to follow what I teach and preach to others. What I didn't realize is what an effective fighting tool this is. By the time I had finished my drive to work, the fight on this front was completely over. I never thought about the situation again from a point of anxiety, and in fact, the Lord gave me strategy in order for the matter to be resolved that day. That is what I call victory!

Notice that Lesson #1, *Rest*, was essential for Lesson #2. I received the bad news of the returned fingerprints late at night. In my flesh, I wanted to figure out everything right then and there. But, I desperately wanted to learn from the Lord and lean into His instruction, so I referred back to Lesson #1 and went to bed. That morning, I was able to pray and meditate with a sound mind—not about the situation—but on who God is. Wisdom helped me understand that if I focused on the wrong thing, then anxiousness and worry would ensue. But if I focused on the Almighty, then faith and fight would arise. Where was my focus going to be?

Philippians 4:8 says:
Finally, brethren, whatever things are true, whatever things are noble, whatever things are just, whatever things are pure, whatever things are lovely, whatever things are of good report, if there is any virtue and if there is anything praiseworthy, meditate on these things.

This also made me think of the story of Peter walking on the water. The disciples had just witnessed the miracle of the feeding of the 5,000. They had more baskets of leftovers than the original basket of food. They were instructed by Jesus to get into the boat and go to the other side. Jesus had taken some time alone to pray, and then He walked on the water to meet the boat. When Peter saw Jesus walking on the water, he said, "Lord, if it is You, command me to come to You on the water." (Matthew 14:28) Jesus invited Peter to come out of the boat, and Peter walked on the water, briefly. But, Peter took his eyes off Jesus and began to be afraid as he focused on the circumstances around him: the wind, the waves Peter began to sink. Peter's focus shifted from the One who was already walking on the water to the circumstances around him. The circumstances could not hold Peter up. They could not save him.

Often, we declare the faithfulness and character of God in church on Sundays, or in our lunches with our brothers and sisters. However, when conflict and injustice are staring us in the face, we choose to focus on the conflict. We choose to meditate on the injustice. But, the victory is not found here. The victory is not in our efforts to dismantle the conflict or to right the wrongs. In fact, these are endless endeavors that never come to a point of conclusion. The enemy, our opponent, would love nothing more than for us to keep our eyes on our circumstances—on what is not going right. If he can keep our focus there, then we will not find rest. We will not seek wisdom or walk in victory. He can gain a foothold in our lives where there is continual anxiety, continual torture, and continual unrest. No, this trial, this fight may not have originated with the enemy, but he will certainly use it to our demise.

Choosing to meditate on the right thing is just that: a choice. If we choose correctly, we have victory. Every time? Yes, every time! Victory is not necessarily that the situation is resolved or justice is found, for circumstances and situations fade, just like everything of this world. The victory is in us—in our ability to walk in the abundant life Jesus offers us in John 10:10. It is in maintaining perfect peace in our minds and hearts, without compromising and without hesitating on what we know is right to do. We can then rest in the Lord and rejoice in Him. Victory is peace. Victory is joy. And, that cannot be taken away by anyone!

The victory is found when we choose to meditate on what is noble, what is just, what is right. The victory is found when we choose to keep our eyes on the Lord and meditate on Him.

This may not be as easy as meditating on something else, but it will effectively annihilate the scheme of the enemy to keep us from a place of victory.

Arise in You

I awake in the morning,
And weighing on me
Are burdens and heaviness
Of what the day brings.

But You have said clearly,
You have commanded indeed,
Not to be anxious or worry
Not to carry these.

So I choose to obey.
I choose Your way.
The burden is on You,
And I hear You say:

"Arise in Me, for this day is new,
You need My strength, to face what's ahead of you.
Be filled with My Spirit, so there is no place
For things you're not to carry, things you're not to embrace."
So I roll to my knees, ask for Your Spirit anew,
And I choose this day to arise in You.

Doubt has no place.
Fear is erased.
As I abide in Your presence,
As I look to Your face

For You have said clearly,
Your Word states the truth:
Meditate on what is worthy,
And what is worthy is You.

I will not walk in the shadows,
I will live in the light.
For here lies are dispelled,
And my heart is made right.

I will speak of Your goodness,
I will proclaim who You are,
As I arise in You this day,
I am safe in Your arms.

Christin Loera (April 14, 2014)

Reflection:

- What are you meditating on when problems surface?

- Where is your focus when faced with a trial?

- How are you finding victory as you are meditating on the Lord in all things?

- What are some of your strategies to make the choice to keep your eyes on Jesus?

Fighting Lesson #3

Don't Be Passive. Don't Be Paralyzed

You know the end is near when you hear, "He has him against the ropes." That phrase signifies that there is one in the boxing match that is either weary or being pummeled, and is about to be knocked out. Being against the ropes is not a good thing—in a boxing match, or in a spiritual fight.

This next fighting lesson did not originate from something that happened to me or my husband with regards to the adoption, but rather from my daily time in the Word and asking the Lord for revelation. This lesson came from Proverbs 24:16, "Though a righteous man falls seven times, he will get up, but the wicked will stumble into ruin."

Often times when we are faced with a trial or with tribulation, we ask, "Can I sit this one out?" or "Why me?" We justify the many reasons why we cannot fight: too tired, too busy, too weak, too frustrated, too angry, too offended. Our thought is if we are forced in the ring, we can simply rest on the ropes and wait it out. Surely God will show up and save us. But up against the ropes is exactly where the enemy wants us, because he knows he can knock us out there.

I think many of us have learned in school the "fight or flight" choice humans make when faced with conflict. From a humanistic perspective, either is fine—it is just in our instinct to do one or the other. From a Christian perspective, there is not a choice. In the book of Esther, when Esther was made Queen, Haman tricked the King into signing (well, Haman signed it on the King's behalf) a law which would allow for the annihilation of the Jewish people on the twelfth day of the month of Adar. Although the wickedness of Haman was revealed to the King, and Haman put to death, it didn't change the fact that on the twelfth day of the month of Adar the Jewish people faced an imminent and deadly threat. The truth was known . . . BUT . . . freedom and life could not be gained just because the truth came to light, and Haman was put to death. No, they still had to fight. The Lord made a way for them to defend themselves and defeat those who wished evil upon them. A new law was written to allow the Jewish people to take up arms on the twelfth day of Adar. They could not stay in bed that day. They had to fight!

Paul says in Ephesians 6 that our fight is not against flesh and blood, but against spiritual powers and principalities. He then encourages us to put on the armor of God. Paul did not give the Ephesian people a choice to be cheerleaders, waterboys, spectators, or fighters. He said we all must put on the armor of God, meaning we all are called to fight. Even in Paul's exhortation in verse 13 that says ". . . and having done all, to stand," the *stand* is not a place of passivity; it is an active verb that encourages us to be ready, to be prepared. Remember, the enemy will attack us whether we want to fight or not.

Yes, we have been called to rest. Yes, we have been encouraged to meditate on the right thing. Both of these can be passive in nature, if we let them be. But in both Lesson #1 and Lesson #2, these are actually active steps we are pursuing for the fight—to fight the fight. Each requires an active choice, and then an active obedience.

Another reaction many have when faced with a trial or tribulation is fear, a fear that is paralyzing. The kind of fear that tells us if we take a step, we're going to be wiped out. The fear that tells us if we take a wrong step, the condemnation of God will fall down on us. This is a paralyzing fear, and we are told not to be paralyzed. In fact, one of the things the Lord spoke to me was this:

Is there someone paralyzed in the trial? Are they seeking My face? I don't leave people paralyzed. I heal lame feet. I show the way out, and I do it with peace and joy.

One of the most beautiful revelations the Lord gave me some years ago was in regard to Abraham. Here was a man who was full of faith, and it was counted to him as righteousness. God declared Abraham righteous because of his faith, not because he did everything right. Abraham had several missteps along the way, from referring to Sarah as his sister (twice, once in Egypt, Genesis 12, and once in Gerar, Genesis 20) and also when trying to fulfill God's promise to him, the promise of a son, in his own strength and reasoning with Hagar. He was not a perfect man, but the Lord saw him as righteous. As New Testament believers, we are made righteous by the blood of Jesus; and while we are not perfect, the Father sees us clothed in the righteousness of Jesus. In other words, I don't have to be perfect. I don't have to take every step without error. What I am asked of the Lord is to do all things with a humble and contrite heart, to seek Him, to listen to Him, to give Him my all—in my heart and in my obedience. This is an issue of the heart. Period.

Isaiah 52:12 says, "For the LORD will go before you, and the God of Israel will be your rear guard." The lie of the enemy is that God is waiting for us to mess up and fail. It is that lie that keeps us in paralyzing fear. The truth, however, is that God is for us. He goes before us and is our rear guard. He watches over us and helps us. He strengthens the weak. If our trust is in anyone but the Lord, if our heart is looking to man to pull us out of crisis or even believing that we must "perform" our way out of crisis, we will be paralyzed. But if we look to the Almighty God, if our eyes are on Him, He says He will never leave nor forsake us.

Here is one thing that should be helpful in identifying what exactly we are fighting, and then moving forward from that point. It is this: trials can come from various sources. There are three questions we must ask when difficulties come (and this came from a brother from Pakistan):

1. Is this from God?
2. Is this from the enemy?
3. Is this a consequence of my sin for which I need to repent?

If it is from God, understand that we are not fighting against God. We are joining Him in His work in us and through us. Transformation from glory to glory and into the image of Jesus doesn't happen while we sleep. It happens through the trial and tribulation. Sometimes it is as simple as learning to wait on Him and His timing. Sometimes it is a much deeper work to remove strongholds and bondages that we have. Whatever it may be, we can be confident that He will complete the good work which He began in us. We must actively pursue the truth, actively trust in Him. Passivity and paralysis will not bring the transforming power of the Lord. And, we don't want to miss the change that only He can bring in our lives!

If it is from the enemy, we must remember that our fight is not against flesh and blood but against powers and principalities. We must actively seek the strategy of the Lord, actively meditate on His word. If we rest against the ropes (passive) or if we sit down on the mat (paralyzed), we will be knocked around. We will be tortured. We will feel defeated. We will lose. To fight (as the Lord wills) will not only bring victory to the situation, but we will be able to walk in the abundant life Jesus offers regardless of the circumstances. What a win!

If it is because of our own sin, we must repent. Repentance is active and is a movement of turning around and walking in the opposite direction. There is nothing passive or paralyzing about repentance; it brings life and restoration.

So we must remember, there is an expectation that the righteous will continue to move forward, even if we stumble, even if we're caught in a trial. Passivity is not an option. Paralysis is not an option. We have to get up. We have to fight.

The Vow

I, Christin Ruth Moore, do take you, Lord, Creator of heaven and earth, Yahweh, to be my God, my Rock and my Salvation. I vow to honor You with my life—my words and deeds. I vow to cherish You—never forgetting Your deep love for me. I vow to praise You in sickness and in health, in times of lack and times of abundance. I vow to serve You with all that I am—I hold nothing back. I vow to take my place as part of the Bride. I vow to love You—unashamed and with abandon. I vow to lay down my flesh, my pride, my will, my wants to Your will, Your desires, Your destiny, and Your purpose. I vow to trust You—to believe that what You say is true and will come to pass. I vow to respect Your power, Your position, and Your place. I vow to put You first—above all—forsaking that which is not from You. You are my Lord. Thank You for choosing me. You are my life. You are my love. For truly one day with You is far greater than a thousand void of You. Neither death, nor things present, nor things to come can separate us. I love you.

Christin Moore (October 29, 2007)

Reflection:

- Is there any place where you are being passive? Is there any place where you are throwing up your hands and giving up?

- If so, what are some strategies the Holy Spirit is wanting to give you in order to walk? In order to fight?

Fighting Lesson #4

Trust

Trust is an easy word to say and an easy lesson to teach, but a very hard thing to walk out. It is very difficult to trust when we are not seeing results, when we are not seeing victory. But Scripture is clear, that we are to trust in a trustworthy God.

Lesson 4 originated from a dream. In the dream, I was at school taking a history class. The professor saw me and told me (and others) that she wanted me to write a paper on an ancient manuscript they had at the school. She took me to a room and pulled out the original manuscripts of 1st and 2nd Peter. I was very excited, as this was a special honor.

The next morning I wrote down the dream, and then read 1 Peter and 2 Peter. It was clear that the Lord was encouraging me to persevere, to continue to trust in Him. At this point in the adoption process, we were waiting for October 30, our next court date—feeling a little helpless, but standing on His word.

Even a few days after the dream and the revelation from 1 Peter and 2 Peter, the Lord was still encouraging me to trust, as evidenced by this journaled conversation I had with Him:

God: "In your time following Me, have you ever regretted where I've taken you?"

Me: No.

God: "Have you been through hard times?"

Me: Yes.

God: "Have you been disappointed with the result?"

Me: No.

God: "Is there any reason to fear My plan?"

Me: No.

God: "Is there any reason to fear October 30?"

Me: No.

God: "I put the fatherless into families, not the other way around."

So there was revelation, there was a word. Was I going to trust? Here's what I learned . . .

1 Peter quotes a lot of the book of Isaiah. Isaiah is so rich in testimony of the Lord—who He is, His saving power, His redeeming power, His compassion, and His love. God proclaims His bigness, His omnipotence, His ability to create, and His ability to break through impossible circumstances. Peter speaks on how we should conduct ourselves as we go through trials, and at the same time reminds us about the character of God toward us. 1 Peter 4:19 says, "So those who suffer according to God's will should, in doing good, entrust themselves to a faithful Creator."

Peter readily admits that there is suffering. In fact, there are no writers of the New Testament that proclaim rainbows and sunshine at all times for believers, but rather they are all very straightforward that we will go through trials, that we will go through tribulations, that there will be suffering. As stated in Lesson #3, we cannot avoid the fight. So, where is the encouragement in this? The reminder that we are in a fight? I think most of us don't need a reminder of our tribulation or trial, but there is so much to be encouraged by when we realize we don't walk through the trials, the tribulations, the suffering alone. The One who is the First and Last knows exactly what we have been through, what we are going through, and even what is ahead of us. He is not going to leave or forsake us (Hebrews 13:5).

In the midst of the trial, tribulation, and suffering, Peter encourages us to entrust ourselves to a "faithful Creator." How does a Creator God fit into a trial? How does a Creator God help us in the fight? God is Creator of all things. As such, He creates the best options for us as we go through trials. He creates a way for us to see His character and move victoriously. And, with each victory, we should come to a deeper level of trust. Our faith is not blind. Our trust is not unsupported. We have faith and trust in a God who is more capable, more wise, more willing to do all that we need. Where there is no way, He "creates" a way. With the utterance of His voice is creation. This is how the impossible becomes possible, because nothing is impossible with Him.

Further encouragement is found in 2 Peter. Peter, in this letter, reiterates 1 Peter, but really emphasizes the impending doom of the wicked. It is easy for us to get lost in the line of thinking that the unjust will never be punished, that they continue in their wickedness, and there won't be justice. We might even think that we may even see victory, but those who deserve punishment will go scot-free. But, this is not what Scripture says. In fact, it is this line of thinking that often erodes our trust in the Lord and ultimately leads us to sinful patterns as we try to make justice happen—wanting to declare judgment on our terms. But there is only one Righteous Judge. In 2 Peter 2:9. it says, " . . . then the Lord knows how to rescue the godly from trials and to keep the unrighteous under punishment until the day of judgment."

In this one verse we learn two things: the Lord knows how to rescue us from trials, and He knows His judgment on the unrighteous. Are we going to lean into Him, are we going to trust Him to rescue us from the trials, to make the way for us to walk them out? And, are we going to let Him be the One that passes judgment? Are we going to trust that He will bring justice in His time and on His terms? I think there could be endless pages written on trusting the Lord for His justice, but it still comes down to one thing: TRUST.

We must trust Him. We must trust He is with us. We must trust He knows every aspect of our situation, and knows with a wisdom beyond what we could ever possess how we are to walk it out for victory. We must trust that He can (and will) make a way where there is no way. We must trust that He will bring justice.

Trusting is not an option. This must be clear in our minds and hearts. Jeremiah 17 talks about the curse and the blessing that comes, depending on who we trust.

The curse (Jeremiah 17:5-6):

> *Thus says the LORD*
> *Cursed is the man who trusts in man*
> *And makes flesh his strength,*
> *Whose heart departs from the LORD.*
> *For he shall be like a shrub in the desert,*
> *And shall not see when good comes,*
> *But shall inhabit the parched places in the wilderness,*
> *In a salt land which is not inhabited.*

The blessing (Jeremiah 17:7-8):

> *Blessed is the man who trusts in the LORD,*
> *And whose hope is the LORD.*
> *For he shall be like a tree planted by the waters,*
> *Which spreads out its roots by the river,*
> *And will not fear when heat comes;*
> *But its leaf will be green,*
> *And will not be anxious in the year of drought,*
> *Nor will cease from yielding fruit.*

If we continue to be obedient to trust, then we will not be anxious; we will not fear, We will be fruitful in every season—even if the season is that of trial, tribulation, or suffering. So, we have to ask ourselves, where (or in whom) is our trust? If in man, we are destined for a curse, for failure. If in God, we are destined for a blessing.

So let us, as it says in Proverbs 3:5-6:
Trust in the Lord with all your heart, and lean not on your own understanding. In all your ways acknowledge Him, and He shall direct your paths.

A Note from the Enemy

I am the one who hates you.

I am the one who would see you destroyed.

I rob what is not mine.

I rob you and then say, "It was never yours," and you believe me.

I rob you and you want it back, and I say "no," and you accept it.

I rob you, and you cry. I laugh.

You blame God and wallow in questions while I make my escape.

I destroy what is not mine.

I destroy your integrity because you locked it out while doing other things.
I destroy your foundation because it is built on preference, emotion, and opinion.
I destroy, and things come crashing down. You are downtrodden, and I am full of glee.
You blame others as your anger arises while I look on in delight.
I kill what is not mine.
I kill your hope because you keep putting it in things or people that can't deliver.
I kill your dreams (this is one of my favorites), by boosting your pride and making everyone else seem foolish.
I kill, and you look inward. You isolate. You self-soothe. And, I have you right where I want you.
You think the answer is found in yourself, and this simply means I can kill pieces of you over and over again.
I steal what is not mine.
I steal your peace and watch you waste time trying to find it.
I steal your joy and mock you as you try to counterfeit it.
I steal these things and leave the morsels of temptation for you to pick up . . . and you do pick them up.
You try every trick in the book to find peace and joy and exhaust yourself. Oh, that makes it so easy to steal again!

I will take truth you have heard, parse it out, wrap it in lies, and feed it to you. Nothing gives me more pleasure for you to take it and say, "Thus sayeth the Lord!"
Ha!
It pleases me to see you "circle the mountain."
It pleases me to see you hopeless.
It pleases me to see you deceived.
It pleases me to see you in despair.
It pleases me to have you search for the answers within yourself, or in nature, or in intellect, or in piety.
Make no mistake, I want to see you destroyed.
I am not your friend.
I am not neutral.
I am your enemy.

A Word from God

I AM.
I am the Way, the Truth and the Life.
I am Love. I love you and have loved you before the foundations of the earth.
I am King of kings, Lord of lords and Ruler over All. All that is on the earth is Mine, all that is in the heavens is Mine, all that is seen and unseen is Mine, and as My child, I say, "ask".
I am Generous. As you ask, I give.
I am There. As you seek, I am found.
I am the Door. As you knock, I open the door.
I am Wisdom. I open to you the door to My heart and My wisdom and My revelation.
I am Mercy. My desire is for you to live an abundant life, full of peace and joy.
I am Joy. Joy is only complete in Me.
I am Peace. Peace is only complete in Me.
I am Provider. I am the source of everything you are in search of, of everything you need.
I am Light. I uncover and dispel the deceit of the enemy.
I am Hope. I am the hope that does not disappoint, that is sure and true.
I am Creator. I speak forth life, and there is life.

I am Restorer. I bring to life things that have been killed, stolen, destroyed.
I am Redeemer. I bought you, paid the price for you, with My precious blood.
I am Life. I bring to life things that previously did not exist.
I am the Banner of Victory. I overcame the enemy. I have already defeated him. I hold the keys to death and Hades.
I am the Lord of All. Nothing the enemy does, or can do—no ploy or scheme is beyond My wisdom, or strength, or knowledge.
I am the Shepherd. I lead you to a place of great fulfillment and destiny.
I am Good. I alone am good, and everything I do is good.
I am the God who sees. I know what you need, when you need it, and how you need it.
I am Sovereign. I have spoken forth My word, and it will accomplish what I intend.
I am the Cornerstone. Let your foundation be in Me; then You will not be shaken.
I am the Rock and Refuge. Let your eyes be on Me, and you will be secure.
I am Almighty God. Let your mind meditate on Me, and you will not be manipulated.

But here is what you must do: Repent. Believe. Follow Me.
Abide in Me. Listen to Me. Obey My words. Have faith in Me.
I am Savior, and behold, I make all things new.
I am Strong and Mighty, and behold, no weapon formed
against you shall prosper.
I am Comforter and Rest, and behold, if you come to Me, you
will find rest.
I am Faithful, Forgiver, Father.
I AM.

Christin Loera (February 22, 2016)

Reflection:

Are there places where you are not fully trusting the Lord? Why not?

Is there a place where you have a misconception about God's character or His love for you?

Where are the places where you have trusted and have seen victory?

Fighting Lesson #5

Love Correction

This next lesson is probably the least fun of all, but at the same time is amazingly revelatory, not only in our walk as a believer, but also in its influence in the fight to bring about growth and victory in the Lord. I say "least fun" because it deals with something none of us want to confront: our lack or our failure; how we missed the mark or didn't get it right. Rare are those who win 100% of the time. With the exception of Jesus, never has there been any who, since birth, got everything right the first time. We inherently know that we will measure up short in some things, yet don't want to hear the instruction or correction that helps us break through to be victorious.

Let me give you a bit of honest insight into my personality. I am a "reformed perfectionist" who prefers to get everything right. (I'm okay with something just less than perfect—that is me—reformed.) I don't want to make a mistake. I try hard to be diligent, to be discerning. I work hard, and I don't quit. I give it "all I have," so if someone tells me that what I have done is not good enough, I am offended and hurt. In fact, if I call my personality what it really is, the perfectionism and the striving is nothing more than pride and self-sufficiency—both rooted in self and both set me up for destruction.

Correction is not something I like, and the Lord knows it; but it is something I desperately NEED. So He, through the Holy Spirit, has been correcting me a lot, and teaching me the benefit of correction.

In this Lesson #5, I would like to offer a new way of looking at correction that is possibly very different from how we have viewed it in the past. From my journal entry on October 18, 2013, I heard the Lord say:

> *Learn to love correction. I correct you so you can fight more effectively, which is often manifested in living day in and day out in an abundance of peace and joy—that zoe—that inheritance that no one can steal. If you hate correction, if you respond poorly to it, then you begin fighting on two fronts—and that means sure defeat. As I said before, I don't correct you because I am vindictive and mean, I correct you because I love you.*

This word, obviously, came right before a word of correction from Him. But what a revelation! In the midst of a fight, we know we are fighting our enemy. We are focused; we are steady; we are strong. But if the Lord brings correction that we don't like, it is easy for us to get frustrated, to get angry, to get down. Think about it: if we are protesting the Lord's correction, then we are basically fighting against the Lord. If we are fighting against the enemy on one side and the Lord on the other, what chance do we have? And, then we must take it one step further. If the Lord knows what we need to be victorious, should we not concede that His correction is His communication of how to be victorious, of what we need when we need it? Why would we fight the correction of the Lord and expect to beat down the enemy? It would be crazy to think that way, yet we so often live this out.

The Lord's correction is meant for my good—to enhance my fighting skills. In Proverbs 3:11-12 it says, "My son, do not despise the chastening of the Lord, nor detest His correction; for whom the Lord loves He corrects, just as a father the son in whom he delights." As a parent, I want my children to learn the best way, the right way. I want to teach them what will help them be healthy, God-fearing, society-contributing adults. I want them to be victorious. The Lord wants nothing less for us.

As with every other lesson, we have to be in a posture to receive the Lord's correction and then be obedient to it. It means we have to be walking in a manner that enables us to hear the voice of the Lord, in humility and submission to His will, and with a singularity of focus on Him for our source of what we need. We have to be able to readily admit that we don't have all of the answers. We must not walk in false humility, but understand that we never have the full picture. We must trust that the Lord is telling us and revealing to us exactly what we need to know. Victory means we must offer ourselves as living sacrifices. We must lay down our flesh, our desires, our preferences, and our chaos for His ways. We must trust and obey. We must let go of our "know-how," and embrace His "this is how."

I love what the Psalmist says in Psalm 144:1: "Blessed be the LORD my Rock, Who trains my hands for war, and my fingers for battle." As His children, the Lord is not about just showering us with blessings and goodness, He is about teaching us and transforming us. He trains us for war. He trains us for battle. He has a direct interest in our lives—the attitude of our heart and how we walk out life—because He has offered us an inheritance that allows us to live in life and light, in peace and joy! He corrects us when we miss the mark in order for us to learn the right way, the wisest way, the victorious way to live.

Learn to love the correction of the Lord. And as a reminder, that correction doesn't always come from Him directly, but it sometimes comes from our spouse, our parent, our pastor, a friend. We need to be vulnerable and humble, knowing that we don't have all of the answers. We don't always know the best way. But if we are willing to learn, to admit our own shortcomings, to listen and embrace correction, and then to obey, we will be victorious EVERY TIME.

To be transparent, my correction which came after that word was on how I was resting. I was trying to figure out the best way for me to rest—even following old patterns of resting—

rather than asking the Lord what would be most restful. I was finding that trying to rest in my own way was not restful at all. But as I listened to His correction and followed His word, I found a true rest that helped me fight as He intended.

The following was written in 2014, and while it doesn't speak of "correction" specifically, it does address the attitude of heart and the obedience that follows. It tells what we must do in order to hear the correction, to be obedient to it, and to walk life out in victory.

The Offering I Choose

Worshipping in the moment, giving my all,
I have often said, "I give you my life."
But as I leave the place,
Where I gave myself to You,
I take me back, and choose exaltation rather than sacrifice.

Too many are the times where I have studied my own self,
Laboring hours over my needs and wants,
How do I look?
And what can I gain?
While You stay in the recesses of my mind.

It is in those moments where I choose the world's kingdom,
I accept what it has to offer me,
A crown of shame
Glory that fades

And all the vileness it has, to be my covering.
It is in those moments where I choose me over You,
I let my folly be my guide.
Destined for sin
Bound by my flesh
I am headed for death, but blinded by pride.

But what You have to offer is far beyond measure,
Your kingdom eternal and alive.
A fullness of life
Victory without question
You offer all for me, if I am willing to sacrifice.

And what You offer is a kingdom of glorious light,
A kingdom that never fades.
With a crown of glory
Adopted as Your own,
If I am willing to give what it takes.

So what is this sacrifice that I am to make?
What offering is pleasing and right?
To lay down my life
To take up my cross,
And to give You first place in my life.

To give You my all and preeminence in my life
May seem a sacrifice too much to maintain.
But compare the eternity
And compare the destiny.
I may lose all of me, but all You are is mine to gain.

Christin Loera (June 4, 2014)

Reflection:

How do you normally receive correction? Well? Poorly?

When you do receive correction, what are some specific steps you can take to process it, accept it, and use it?

Are you praying for your heart to learn to love correction?

Fighting Lesson #6

Stay Present

At this point we are close to our court date, less than two weeks away. I have heeded the Lord; I have listened to His instruction, but the enemy never stops. Thoughts keep coming at me, and I can't seem to escape. What if they split up the boys? What if the judge has a lapse of wisdom and actually favors with the other side? What if we lose them both—we've been their parents for almost two years now? I am trying to take every thought captive unto obedience to the Lord, knowing the importance of doing so. And with my pursuit of obedience, He reveals something new.

On October 22, 2013, I felt the Lord say:

> *Be in the present. Don't give yourself to daydreams or fantasy. If you do not take those thoughts captive, then you can end up fighting the "not yet" or the "not ever" rather than the battle that is before you. Letting your mind wander may be escape for the moment, but it does not remove you from the reality of a fight, and will put you in a place where fighting is more difficult.*

And there it was . . . I must continue, no matter how many thoughts had to be taken captive, no matter how many times

I had to do it. That was time and energy well-spent. That was time and energy that was fruitful. But, it wasn't just about taking thoughts captive. It was about taking the thoughts captive AND staying in the present moment so I could be about the work the Lord called me to do that very day. The flip side would be to daydream—to fantasize—to even have conversations/confrontations in my mind with people that I never met, spewing anger and frustration if the verdict of the Judge did not go our way. Talk about a waste of energy, waste of time, waste of emotion, and yes, waste of brain power. It was that "what if" road that would lead to nowhere and could have taken me in endless loops and emotional highs and lows, never producing anything but anxiety, worry, and fear. To me, there was only one clear path to walk.

In a fight, you have to know your enemy. You have to give yourself to the One who has defeated the enemy. The One that will defeat him! To waste time thinking of things that may never happen means you have taken your MIND, your HEART, and your SPIRIT out of the fight. Quite frankly, it means you are taking your focus off of the Lord. Understand—your mind, heart, and spirit might be taken out of the fight, but the fight still rages. The enemy doesn't see that you need a "time out" and a period to adjust. He doesn't say "okay—I'll give you some space. You look like you need a minute." If he sees you step out in any capacity (such as by not staying present), he is going in to do damage, which only makes the fight that much more difficult.

There is a reason we are commanded to "Love the Lord with all of your heart, mind, soul, and strength." (Deuteronomy 6:3) Our mind cannot be disengaged, our heart cannot be distracted, and our spirit will be ready and willing *if* our heart is full of faith, peace, and joy. Either we are all in, focused on the Lord, or we are not engaging fully and effectively. Three things we must do as we remain present:

1. **Take thoughts captive**. Begin to recognize thoughts that are not of the Lord, that are not helpful. Lay those at the feet of Jesus, and then choose to engage your mind, spirit, and emotion on what is right before you.

2. **Meditate on Scripture.** Read, and memorize the written Word, and keep in front of you what God has spoken. To me it was that these boys were ours, and there was plenty of Scripture that God had given to confirm His promise.

3. **Give ourselves to prayer and praise.** Have others praying with you. Putting the Lord in His proper place as we humbly approach Him keeps us from being carried away with things that are "not yet" or "not ever."

To stay in a posture of faith and obedience, our minds have to be engaged, listening to the Holy Spirit. Our minds cannot be wandering, but must be intentionally focused. Have you ever said "I'm having a night off to just veg-out in front of the t.v.?" Did you end that time full of hope and clarity? My thought is "no." You must meditate on the present, let go of focusing on circumstances, and stop yourself from scripting conversations in your mind. You have to be intentional to stay present.

This lesson is closely intertwined with Lesson #2, "Choose to Meditate on the Right Thing." So, I can either choose to meditate on the "not yet" or "not ever," or I can meditate on the present. If I choose the "not yet" or "not ever," I am swinging at the air. I am fighting a fight that hasn't even started, or maybe will never happen. What a waste of energy and emotion! And then, as in Lesson #2, if I choose the present, I can either go to 1) distraction, 2) my circumstances, or 3) God and who He is.

I am thankful I did not waste time on doubt or the fear of "what if we had to split up the boys," etc. I was able to partner with my husband to pastor those we were called to shepherd. I was able to submit the issues of others before the Lord, and listen for the words God would speak in their situations. The waste of time would have affected not only me, but many others.

A word of warning: The enemy loves—I mean loves—to get our eyes off of the Lord and to get them on ourselves. If our eyes turn to ourselves, we immediately lose perspective, we immediately lose hope, and we immediately lose joy and peace. I am not saying there is not a place for Holy Spirit-led introspection. We need to be honest with ourselves before the

Lord, but at all times, keeping our eyes—our identity—on Him and in Him. If we allow self-focus to rule our thoughts, it is destructive to our spirit; and the enemy knows that. He will use every place and every opportunity to shift the focus of our eyes. When we stay focused, though, here is what can happen: A few days later, still being honest before the Lord but looking to Him, I heard Him say:

> *My verdict has been handed down. My verdict was spoken before the establishment of the world. What I have spoken, no man can thwart. Take hold of this in faith. Trust Me.*

Yes! So instead of being discouraged, without hope, or robbed of peace and joy, I left my time with the Lord encouraged, hopeful, full of joy and peace, and ready to face the day!

But seek first the kingdom of God and His righteousness, and all these things shall be added to you. Therefore do not worry about tomorrow, for tomorrow will worry about its own things. Sufficient for the day is its own trouble.
(Matthew 6:33-34)

Wandering Eyes

Why do I let my eyes wander?
To what advantage is there to take my eyes off You?

When I take my eyes off You . . .

I can look at my neighbors and see their pain.
Seeing their pain brings my own pain before me.
I choose to meditate on the hurt.
My eyes are on me once again,
And I see how wounded I am.

I can look at strangers and see their injustice.
Seeing their cause brings my own injustice before me.
I choose to count all of the wrongs.
My eyes are on me once again,
And I see how unfair life has been.

My eyes wander to the hopelessness that is in the world.
Seeing the doom set before the world unveils my broken dreams.
I choose to dwell in "if only."
My eyes are on me once again,
And I see self-preservation as necessity.

But, when I keep my eyes on You . . .

But, when I look at You,
I see my Healer, who binds my wounds.
I see my Righteous Judge, who defends my life.
I see my All in all, in whom my identity is found.

But, when I look to You,
I see my Source of hope.
I see justice as the noon day.
I see a restoration.

And as my eyes remain fixed on You,
I see in my reflection a child of God, whole and complete, fully loved and fully cared for.

Lord, let my eyes wander no more,
But let them stay on You.

Christin Loera (February 6, 2017)

Reflection:

When things get tough, when you are going through a trial, are you keeping your focus on the Lord?

Do you have a tendency to daydream or script conversations?

What are some real strategies you can apply to keep your mind from wandering?

Fighting Lesson #7

Become Undignified

I am months into this fight. I am pursuing the Lord; I am being corrected; I am being transformed; I am taking thoughts captive; I am resting, and I am remaining present. But, there is one more thing that I know I must do—praise. So here is my human dilemma: I actually am not downtrodden every second of the day. I am hopeful. The Lord is speaking to me, and my trust in Him is growing day by day. I feel peace. I feel love and gratitude in my heart. In fact, thanksgiving is bursting out . . . but I feel that if I praise the Lord as He calls me to do, people will interpret that as me being unaware of the seriousness of this trial.

I love the story of David bringing the ark of the covenant to the City of David in 2 Samuel 6. It says in verse 16 that he was "leaping and whirling before the Lord." His heart was so full of gratitude, love, and thanksgiving to the Lord, that David danced with all his might. But, not everyone was pleased. It says of David's wife, Michal, that she "despised him in her heart" (2 Samuel 6:16). Michal confronted David, ashamed of how he humbled himself in front of the people. But David would have none of it. He said, "It was before the Lord . . . And I will become even more undignified than this, and will be humble in my own sight" (2 Samuel 6:21-22).

If I worship as David did before the Lord, I am certain to be chastised by the "Michals" in my life, who don't understand that this is a key component of walking out a trial in our inheritance as children of God, regardless of the circumstances. Yes, this is my human dilemma, because there is no spiritual dilemma. My spirit knows it is right to exalt and praise God. My life is an offering of praise before the Lord. The Lord is due my praise and thanksgiving at every moment of every day, no matter what is going on around me. So, really there's no dilemma at all. I will praise, regardless of what anyone else says or thinks. Now, if I could only let myself become more undignified!

Reading from Psalm 106, verse 2 struck me in a new way. It says, "Who can utter the mighty acts of the Lord? Who can declare all His praise?" From there, my heart poured out before the Lord in my journal:

Often as I praise You, my heart is flooded with emotion and gratitude. I lift up praise as I know how, but it isn't enough— not full enough, not rich enough—to express the worthiness of You, to express Your majesty and glory, Your honor and power, Your goodness and faithfulness, and Your love. Truly, who can declare Your mighty acts, and who can proclaim all the praise due You? My words fall short. My sentiments cannot carry my heart's praise. I am only a human, praising an eternal, sovereign God. Are there words in heaven adequate enough? Or, will I spend eternity unable to fully express to You who You are to me?

Praise and thanksgiving is not a recommendation, but rather a command of the Lord. From Psalm 106, "Oh, give thanks to the Lord, for He is good! For His mercy endures forever," to Psalm 146, "One generation shall praise Your works to another, and shall declare Your mighty acts," to Philippians 4, "Rejoice in the Lord always. Again I will say, rejoice!" to James 1, "Count it all joy when you fall into various trials," and again in 1 Peter 4, "Rejoice to the extent you partake in Christ's sufferings, that when His glory is revealed, you may also be glad with exceeding joy."

We are to rejoice in the trial and rejoice in the victory! Rejoice that our faith is being tested. Rejoice that our God has an opportunity to prove Himself mighty. Praise the One that gives us a Word to stand on that will not return void. Give thanks to the One Who is faithful, even if we are not. Let our praise— the sound of my voice, the sound of your voice—be lifted up to the Most High God. Let us not hold back. Let us not be distracted, concerned with the opinion of others or fearful. Let us praise with reckless abandon!

Oh, and this is not just a one-time event, or an every Sunday moment. Thanksgiving and praise should never cease to be on our lips, as they should be an overflow of our heart. In fact, praise and thanksgiving are not about making God feel good about Himself. It's not about feeding His ego. He doesn't need us to praise Him in order for Him to know who He is. He doesn't need our affirmation. He has always been and always will be omniscient, omnipotent, omnipresent God Almighty. But here is what praise and thanksgiving do: they turn our heart's and mind's focus on the One who can do the impossible, who is the same yesterday, today, and forever. But even more than putting our attention and focus on who He is, thanksgiving and praise bring forth remembrance. Offering praise and thanksgiving helps us to remember what He has already done for us. It tears down the circumstances that vie for our attention and replays victory after victory He has brought us to, keeping that at the forefront. As we bring attention to Him and what He has done, our hope rises, our joy increases, our countenance brightens, and our peace is solidified. So with every door that is opened because of our trial, we can walk through with praise and thanksgiving, without thought or fear of what man might think or say, giving God all the glory. We can truly be rejoicing all the time!

On the flip side, if we become bogged down in the emotion that equates to the severity of our circumstances, we will not be praising. That is what the enemy is after. He is after us to stay focused on what is wrong, where we lack, or why we are in this place. He wants our hearts to stay sorrowful and silent. The enemy wants to steal, kill, and destroy (John 10:10). But, we are called to the abundant life. So how do we fight? We must walk in the spirit opposite of what our enemy wants us to feel. When we praise, we are declaring that victory is imminent. If we do not praise, we tell our enemy we have conceded defeat.

Our praise and thanksgiving are not to be between just us and the Lord, within the confines of our room. It is to be shared! It is to be spread! We are commanded to tell the generations of His good works. It should not be a "by the way" or "just thought you should know" topic. It should be "I can't wait to tell you what the Lord is doing!" Let excitement rise. Let His joy be evident. Don't be silent!

Here is one more personal application that I felt was part of this lesson. I believe there is more to being "undignified" than just in praise and thanksgiving. What is the testimony on my lips? Am I willing to talk of faith, *my faith*? Am I willing to look like a fool for Christ? Am I ready to have unbelievers (and possibly believers as well) judge me to be a little crazy? Am I willing to talk about the words the Lord has given to me, how I am standing in faith, EVEN BEFORE the victory is seen? I learned a great deal in this area during this trial. I learned how to speak the words in faith—sharing that faith and telling people that God is faithful—before the trial was over. The amazing thing is that I shared faith, and then everyone who heard was able to see it happen.

The world calls for modesty in all things—moderation is best. I do not want to be modest when talking about my Savior and

God. He should not be presented as One who wears a suit and tie, but as One who is sitting on the throne in all majesty, all glory, all holiness and righteousness, in all splendor. He is worthy of all of our praise!

Let no one deceive himself. If anyone among you seems to be wise in this age, let him become a fool that he may become wise. For the wisdom of this world is foolishness with God. (1 Corinthians 3:18-19)

The following was written over a year before we adopted our children. It was an act of faith . . . and it did come to pass.

Bountifully

I will sing praise to the Lord, for He has dealt bountifully with me.
Let the barren one rejoice,
For in the Father's voice,
Is the creation of all new and living things.

Let the barren one rejoice,
For in the Father's voice,
He has dealt bountifully with me.

I will sing praise to the Lord, for He has dealt bountifully with me.
Though my human flesh will fail,

By the cross and resurrection He prevailed,
Over sin and death and gives me victory.

Though my human flesh will fail,
By the cross and resurrection He prevailed,
For He has dealt bountifully with me.

I will sing praise to the Lord, for He has dealt bountifully with me.
Though my sacrifice seem small,
Let me sacrifice my all,
That His glory may be revealed to humanity.

Though my sacrifice seem small,
Let me sacrifice my all,
For He has dealt bountifully with me.

Declare His good works to all the nations.
Speak His goodness to all generations.
Sing His praise and bless the name of the Lord,
His truth and mercy are forevermore.

I will sing praise to the Lord, for He has dealt bountifully with me.
My heart cannot contain,
The praises due His name,
For You, my Lord, have dealt bountifully with me!

Christin Loera (January 31, 2011)

Reflection:

How do you reconcile in your heart the victory you do not yet see with the current circumstances?

Are you willing to praise even though you don't see the victory yet?

What is the overflow of your heart during a trial?

Are you experiencing peace and joy? Is there guilt associated with that?

What can you do to walk in praise and thanksgiving when everything around you speaks to the contrary?

Fighting Lesson #8

Delay is not Defeat
(In fact, delay is not even delay.)

The day had come—October 30. It was time for the trial. Our case would go before a judge, and he or she would determine the outcome of where our children would be—with us or with someone they didn't know. We had been prepped by our lawyer. We had worked through the questions that would be asked of us. We were prayed up. We were geared up. We were ready for the fight. We were ready with the hosts of angels behind us . . . and then we get the call. There would be no fight today. While we knew we physically didn't have to be present before the judge, we were under the impression we would receive a call for questions. However, no one informed our attorney or us that there was a specific way to call in to the courtroom, and because we had not done it the correct way, there would be another continuance.

At that point I did the most mature and spiritual thing in the world . . . I sat on the floor and cried. Actually, I sobbed. It was that ugly cry where tears are streaming, where you are so loud wailing, but no one can comprehend what you are saying. That is, no one but God.

There were so many thoughts racing through my mind, one being "Why is this DELAYED?" I was defining the continuance as delay. I was thinking there might be a wrinkle in the game plan—the plan of attack, but how could that be since God had given me such a powerful word the morning before, a word of sure victory? How could He let this happen? (Here is the word He gave in Lesson #6:

My verdict has been handed down. My verdict was spoken before the establishment of the world. What I have spoken, no man can thwart. Take hold of this in faith. Trust in Me. You will win this time. You will win the appeal. The adoption will be completed. I will bring this to completion.)

It is often in these moments where you feel the tenderness of the Father. He saw every tear I shed. He heard every question I asked. He had the answer and comfort I needed. He had not misspoken to me the day before. It was my understanding and perspective that needed to be changed. I heard Him say:

My timing is always right. You do not see the things I do. In fact I already see how everything has played out. You have to trust that I know what I am doing . . . because I do.

How often have I not only questioned the Lord's timing, but I have said "He is delayed!" I have somehow determined I have the better plan. I know the full strategy. I have my word to stand on, and I know how it will play out. But, what I really do is set myself up for disappointment—disappointment in the Lord and disappointment that I somehow failed spiritually. What I need is a correction in my thinking. I put the Lord's ability to act in the situation on my timeline. I do not recognize His sovereignty. I do not recognize His position as Lord over all. I do not see how selfish I am. Yes—I said it—selfish. If I want the Lord's will, but in my time, I'm walking in selfishness. If I want the Lord's will, but I expect it to play out in life a certain way, I'm walking in selfishness. If I'm injecting any part of me, my thoughts, or my perception into what the Lord is doing, then I'm injecting my self-will, self-trust, self-knowledge, and self-sufficiency. In short, I'm being selfish.

The Lord does not see us standing in the trial and say "Oh, let's see how he or she figures out how to make it work, how to move My heart." No. The Lord has seen the trial coming since the beginning of time, and He knows the absolute best way through it, with everything He intends to be accomplished. The best thing we can do is rest in the Lord and trust His timing, trust His strategy. The Lord's timing is right and perfect. We can trust it. We can bet on it. We can hope in it. One thing is for certain: He is always doing more than we know or can comprehend.

At the end of the trial, I understood why each continuance was necessary. For the miraculous to occur, for the heart of the birthfather and his attorney to change, time was a necessity. I do not know, nor will I fully know on this side of heaven, what happened to change his heart, but I know something did happen. Within two months between hearings, he went from a "win-at-all-costs" attitude, including contacting the birth mother's family so her family could harass her, to laying down his parental rights, just needing to know we would provide a few years of confirmation that the boys were okay. Was it a dream? A vision? A softening of his heart? Only God knows. From a blindness caused by pride and arrogance to a release of what was his only bargaining chip. ONLY God's hand could have done it!

Now I testify to the perfection in His timing. A battle won without a fight could only be won in His perfect time!

Hebrew 2:8 says:
You have put all things in subjection under his feet." For in that He put all in subjection under him, He left nothing that is not put under him. But now we do not yet see all things put under him.

We do not know all things He is doing, battles He is fighting, victories He is winning.

Psalm 112:7-8 also provided great encouragement:
He will not be afraid of evil tidings; His heart is steadfast, trusting in the LORD. His heart [is] established; He will not be afraid, Until he sees [his desire] upon his enemies.

The Lord is victorious. The Lord is worthy of our trust. His mighty hand and outstretched arm will always find us.

The following was written the day prior to the day we were supposed to have the trial, which ended up in continuance. I felt the Spirit speak this to my spirit during a time of praise and worship. A feeling of sure victory washed over me. While I had a "moment" upon hearing about the continuance, this was a word I clung to for the remainder of the process.

Victorious

The battle lines are drawn
The time is set to fight.
But as I go out ready
The enemy's been set to flight.

With Your mighty arm and hand
You defeated every foe
So out of my heart and mouth
Let Your praises flow.

I heard You do this in old,
and I see You do it now.
I feel Your love and mercy
as Your matchless power comes down.

God over all creation
Lord over great and small
All You do is speak Your voice
And every enemy falls.

The battle lines are drawn
The time is set to fight
But with You I stand victorious
The enemy must run from Your light.

Christin Loera (October 29, 2013)

Reflection:

If you have put the Lord's will on your timeline, why?

How can you recognize the Lord's sovereignty, even in a trial?

Are there places where you feel the Lord doesn't see and might let something drop?

And how is that driving your own solutions and actions rather than resting in the Lord?

If there is delay (in your view), do you wait on the Lord? Or worry?

Fighting Lesson #9

Our Most Powerful Weapon: The Word of God

This lesson did not come with some great dramatic event, but rather in the quiet stillness of a peaceful night. This lesson is a reminder that the enemy is searching for a foothold somewhere, really anywhere he can get it. We have to be on guard for all things. Even if you feel you are solid in your faith for a situation, be ready for the enemy to go after your relationships, your finances, or anything, because the enemy will do whatever he can to get you sidetracked and sideways.

In the middle of a sound night's sleep, I woke up and began to have a barrage of thoughts against my husband. I wasn't pondering any conversation we had the day before. I wasn't thinking about our family or us as a couple. There was no ramp up to it. Like going from 0 to 60 in 2.5 seconds, that really is what it felt like as these thoughts began to enter my mind. It was accusation after accusation. It was criticism after criticism. My husband was not making the right decisions for us financially. He was not leading us to a place of prosperity. He was letting things drop. I could feel myself becoming more and more anxious. Now, not able to go back to sleep, I had a choice. I could entertain the accusations. I could wake my husband up and berate him with these accusations, or I could speak truth to them. In that moment, I prayed out to God that I would stay focused on Him, His provision, and how He is my sure rock. And, it wasn't just a simple prayer, I really was crying out to the Lord. I desperately wanted those thoughts to stop. I desperately wanted the accusations to cease.

The next morning, the Holy Spirit reminded me of a Scripture—a simple verse—"Not that we are sufficient of ourselves to think of anything as being from ourselves, but our sufficiency is from God." (2 Corinthians 3:5) And with that, all feelings of anxiety, frustration, irritation, etc. left. That was it. Done. They did not return. I experienced that level of complete peace one other time, and that was during Lesson #2.

From journal entry 12/27:
Lord, You have been faithful to me. You have shown me Your love time and time again. With a single reminder of Your word, you crushed the enemy's attempts to harass me. That is how powerful Your word is. I am amazed at how definitive, how complete, how absolute it is in the midst of battle. Let me not voluntarily come under torment again. Let me stand and fight, not crouch and cover my face. I truly feel like I can soar in those moments—as it brings a fruit of peace. Praise be to Your Name.

If I let it, the power of the Word of God can crush—obliterate—my enemy's attempt to distract me, thwart the advancement, sidetrack my emotion, and steal my inheritance. A single verse with so much power and authority is indescribable. In one moment, accusation, and in the next, peace. There was no more fighting. There was no more wrestling with thoughts on which I shouldn't dwell. It was done. It was complete. The Lord was victorious.

Hebrews 4:12 tells us:
For the word of God is living and powerful, sharper than any double-edged sword, piercing even to the division of soul and spirit, and of joints and marrow, and is a discerner of the thoughts and intents of the heart.

Most of us have learned this verse from an early age, or at least have heard it mentioned on numerous occasions during Sunday morning sermons. There is a reason for that—it is true, and it really is the most powerful weapon we have.

I believe the enemy wants to say that the verse is just words, that the Bible is just words. The words may tell a story, but they are not powerful. They certainly cannot bring freedom and tear down strongholds. The words can bring wisdom, but they are nothing more than head knowledge. Brothers and sisters, this is the biggest lie we could believe. How could it be that the inspired Word of God would not have power? How could it be that the One whose very breath is a life-giving, life-creating force would not breathe life into us through His Word?

Of course, we all have our habits of how we operate. We all have our modus operandi, developed by genetics, environment, and past experience. We go through our analysis, our evaluation, we weigh the options, and we make a decision based on our assumed conclusions. In reality, though, there is a single source that truly can address every trial we face, that can give us a more accurate picture of who our true enemy is, what he is truly after, who our Father is, what He is capable of, and what He can do. You see, our circumstances will change from week to week, month to month, year to year, but there are foundational truths to which we can cling that do not change: our salvation in Christ; the fact that Jesus Christ is the same yesterday, today, and forever (Hebrews 13:8); that we cannot comprehend the vastness of the Father's love for us; that He knows our every need and will provide for it; that His Word is truth; and it goes on and on. So no matter our circumstances, we can hold firm to the truth of the Word, and rest, knowing that He will provide a way where there seems to be no way. He is, after all, the Master of Breakthroughs (2 Samuel 5:20).

But there is one more thing we HAVE to remember: not only do we have our sword of the Spirit (Ephesians 6:17), which is the Word of God, as our weapon, but we have the authority to use it. We have been given every right and privilege associated with being in the body of Christ and being empowered by the Holy Spirit. What amazing strength we have when we wield that Sword! Oh, how that Sword can slay the intents of the enemy, can stop the destruction of the enemy, and can also heal and build up in truth and love.

Now, I must remember that I carry that authority, and this is how the Word of God should operate every day! This isn't just for a trial: this is for life!

My Shield, on the following page, is based on what Scriptures tell me about my God, because I do not want to ever, ever, ever forget.

Christin Loera (January 7, 2017)

My Shield. My Protector. The One Who Defends me from the attack of the enemy. The One Who Created me and formed me, Who knows what is best for me. The One Who teaches, stretches, corrects me so that I may be all He has called me to be. The One Who never leaves me nor forsakes me, whether in peace or in the battle. The One Who knows my vulnerabilities, Who has already won the victory and leads me to victory. The One Who sees the upright of heart. The One Who blesses the righteous and surrounds them with favor. The One Who is my glory and the lifter of my head. The One Who has removed any reason for fear, in whom I can rest and have peace. The One Who made a way to Him when there was no way. The One Who leads and guides me down the path, during times of peace or times of difficulty. The One Who answers when I knock. The One Who provides when I ask. The One Who reveals when I seek. The One Who has declared this is the day of salvation. The One Who sees and meets me. The One of great compassion and mercy, whose lovingkindness never fails. The One whose Word does not, nor will ever return void. The One Who is constant—the same yesterday, today, and forever. The One in whom I can put my complete trust. Great is Your Name, O Lord! You are great and greatly to be praised! How marvelous are Your works! How beautiful is Your creation! How majestic is Your Name in all of the earth. All praise is due Your Name. All honor, glory, power, and majesty be unto You! You alone are the King of kings and the Lord of lords. You are Faithful and True. All Your words are righteous and pure. You are holy! There is no deceit found in You. There is no injustice or evil in You. You are the Spotless Lamb, the Perfect Sacrifice, and I owe You my life and my all. Let us worship the Lord—Maker of heaven and earth! Let us lift up praise to the object of our affection and love—the Lord our God! Let Your praises never cease to be on our lips and thanksgiving in our heart. Thank You, Lord! You are good! Your love will never cease. Your kindness will never end. Let me give praise to the One Who holds me, Who protects me, Who is my All in all. Thank You. I give my praise to You. With all that I am, be praised and magnified. I love You, Lord!

Reflection:

What are some Scriptures from the Word that have encouraged you in a trial?

What are some other Scriptures you feel you need to meditate on in order to learn them, and then use them as a weapon?

How is memorizing the Word important? Do you believe it's important?

Commit to memorizing more Scripture so that you can recall it when you—or someone else—might need it!

Fighting Lesson #10

HUMILITY. HUMILITY. HUMILITY . . . IT WASN'T ME!

God wins! While I could stop there, I'll give you the details on how this ended.

On January 10, 2014, our case finally came before a Judge. The case was tried in California, but my husband and I were able to stay in Tennessee and call in (as directed, of course).

10:25 a.m.	We call in and are on the "court call."
10:45 a.m.	Our case is called. I have knots in my stomach, but I'm still confident. Again, we have been prepared by our lawyer, and we know the Holy Spirit will help us answer any question that comes our way. HOWEVER, the birthfather has not been transported from jail, so the Judge says our case will be heard once he arrives.
10:50 a.m. - 1:00 p.m.	We hear other cases while staying on the phone, including another case to relinquish paternal rights,

1:00 p.m.   Court recess

1:10 p.m.   The Judge now calls our case. (Deep sigh) We hear our attorney say to the Judge that she has been approached with a deal that she needs to discuss with the petitioners (us).
The Judge calls for a recess until 1:30 p.m.

1:15 p.m.   We receive a call from our attorney. She tells us that at 1:08 p.m. she was approached by the birthfather's attorney and said (in my paraphrase): "You may win today, or I might be able to get this stretched out for six more months, but my client is willing to make a deal." The birthfather was willing to relinquish his rights, including any right to appeal, if we sent updates to him on the boys.

During this time, my husband was texting for counsel. We felt good about it, but wanted to make sure the birth mother was okay with it, as she had been so supportive from the beginning. The birth mother said she was fine with the arrangement.

A deal was reached.

1:30 p.m.   The Judge recalls everyone. For the next ten minutes, both attorneys go over the deal with the Judge. He agrees. He signs the order.

1:40 p.m.   It is finished!

The Lord was true to His word:

> ***You will have victory.***
> ***My arm is not too short.***
> ***My hand has not grown weak.***
> ***My voice is not silent.***
> ***I am Almighty God.***

And with that, our battle was over! There was praise and exaltation to the Lord, a lot of texts and phone calls . . . and a trip to Chuck E. Cheese!

The lesson here was a very important one. With victory can come a place of pride. This place can look any number of ways, such as:

- I made it through my battle/trial, and you can make it through yours because yours isn't as bad as mine.

- I kept the faith, why can't you?

- God did this because I was so good and devoted to Him.

- Now that I have moral authority, let me tell you what you're doing wrong.

A victory has to be walked out in humility. Victory doesn't mean I'm any better, smarter, or more worthy. **Victory is simply the expected outcome because we serve Almighty God, and we have chosen to follow in faith and obedience to His direction.**

The enemy, however, would love for that pride to sneak its way in. In fact, often with success comes a place of vulnerability. This is a place where the enemy can come in and steal the thankfulness and gratefulness of the heart. When those are stolen, pride and arrogance can march right in and set up shop in your heart. And when pride and arrogance are the attitude, self sufficiency is right behind, ready to take its place on the throne of your heart.

We have to stay humble. There is no way around it. Philippians 2:5-9 talks about the humility of Jesus, and truly that is our example to follow. Humility is not a weakness, but rather a confidence in the Lord, in His works and character, rather than the confidence in our own self.

Although already mentioned in Lesson #5, I love what Psalms 144:1-2 says:
Blessed be the LORD my Rock, Who trains my hands for war, And my fingers for battle—My Lovingkindness and my For-

tress, My High Tower and my Deliverer, my Shield and the One in whom I take refuge, Who subdues my people under me.

He trains us for battle, but the victory is His. It is He who subdues people under us. It is He who is our Fortress, Deliverer, and Shield. He may train us, but He has won!

Another encouragement to stay humble comes from Psalm 108:12-13, which reminds us that it really is the Lord who brings the victory. "Give us help from trouble, for the help of man is useless. Through God we will do valiantly, for it is He who shall tread down our enemies."

When the trial is over, I recite what I learned; I teach what I experienced; I rejoice in the Lord, but I cannot rest in the victory. This is not the last battle, trial, or persecution I will face. Nor is this the last victory of my life. There is always opposition of the enemy, but where there is opposition, there is a way of salvation. We must continue to fight!

Therefore I must keep my eyes on Jesus—in the good and the bad—no matter what comes my way. He is still my life source, and He is the only one that makes for a sure victory. I must, as Scripture says in John 15:4-5:
Abide in Me, and I in you. As the branch cannot bear fruit of itself, unless it abides in the vine, neither can you, unless you abide in Me. I am the vine, you are the branches. He who

abides in Me, and I in him, bears much fruit; for without Me you can do nothing.

Even though this poem was written years later, it still expresses where my hope lies, and where I know I will see my victory.

On My Behalf

A wall is set before me,
A mountain I cannot climb.
My only hope is in Your power,
For mine is lacking every time.

I cannot control the universe
Or where circumstances may land.
But I can find rest and peace in You,
And find deliverance in Your mighty hand.

I have seen the valley of the shadow of death,
I have felt the pain, despair, and hurt;
But oh, the joy it is to my soul
When I see Your hand at work.

For nothing is impossible for You;
You make dry bones live again.
You make a way where there is no way,
Out of certain death, You breathe life within.

Oh let my eyes never fail to see
Or my heart never fail to believe.
There is One who gives abundantly
If I am open and ready to receive.

Oh let my faith grow ever more and more
And let my soul never forget
Your power, Your might, Your glory
All at work on my behalf.

Christin Loera (June 13, 2015)

Reflection:

What emotions have you wrestled with after a victory?

How do you remain thankful and grateful . . . and humble?

How does this strengthen your faith and testimony?

Fight On

Conclusion

I hope these lessons have been an encouragement to you. There is so much that could be expanded on for each point. As a pastor I could definitely go on and on, but that is not really the point of this book.

I believe the Lord is going to show each of you how to fight the battles before you in a way that is unique to you. These points simply highlight the character of the Lord, the truth of the Word, and give testimony of how the Lord worked through these things with me to give you hope. Everything the Lord said came to pass. Every word He spoke, He fulfilled. He is trustworthy. He is faithful. And, He wants to be the same to you.

We are children of an amazing God. As believers in Christ, we have an unfair advantage. That's not to say that all things will go our way, and everything will work out as miraculously as this particular trial did. But, I know that I know the Lord will never leave us or forsake us. I would be remiss if I didn't acknowledge that it doesn't always turn out well. The marriage might not be saved; the loved one might die from the sickness; you might not get the dream job. But the important thing to remember is that this is not about the circumstantial result. **This is about you finding, receiving, walking in, and dwelling in God's best for you in the midst of even the worst of circumstances**. He doesn't drop us off and hope we do everything right. He is right there. He is waiting to give you wisdom, peace, joy and hope, even when circumstances around you seem horrible. Our hope is not in what happens or doesn't happen. Our hope is in the One who holds us, provides for us, comforts us, hears us, instructs us, and loves us. We can find His best for us. We can live His best for us. But most importantly, He is wanting to transform us into Christ's image—molding our character, sifting our heart, making us into something beautiful.

One more nugget I believe the Lord wants me to share is that it is really easy to get self-absorbed during a trial. It is easy to make things all about us, and what we are going through. But, we all know there are others in our life who are going through their own trials. Life doesn't stop. Life isn't paused. It continues, even in the midst of our trial. So be aware and continue to make the choice to be available to be used by God, however He needs you—offering an encouraging word to others, a listening ear to someone in need, and a place of compassion for the hurting. The moment you make it all about you is the moment you will lose perspective. And once you lose perspective, you lose hope, you lose peace, and you lose joy. Let's be on guard so that does not happen to us!

I've added Psalm 25, which gives us insight to David's heart-cry, and which I believe, if it is the cry of our heart, the Lord will honor, bless, and fulfill.

> *A Psalm of David. To You, O LORD, I lift up my soul. O my God, I trust in You; Let me not be ashamed; Let not my enemies triumph over me. Indeed, let no one who waits on You be ashamed; Let those be ashamed who deal treacherously without cause. Show me Your ways, O LORD; Teach me Your paths. Lead me in Your truth and teach me, For You are the God of my salvation; On You I wait all the day. Remember, O LORD, Your tender mercies and Your lovingkindnesses, For they are from of old. Do not remember the sins of my youth, nor my transgressions; According to Your mercy remember me, For Your goodness' sake, O LORD. Good and upright is the LORD; Therefore He teaches sinners in the way. The humble He guides in justice, And the humble He teaches His way. All the paths of the LORD are mercy and truth, To such as keep His covenant and His testimonies. For Your name's sake, O LORD, Pardon my iniquity, for it is great. Who is the man that fears the LORD? Him shall He teach in the way He chooses. He himself shall dwell in prosperity, And his descendants shall inherit the earth. The secret of the LORD is with those who fear Him, And He will show them His covenant. My eyes are ever toward the LORD, For He shall pluck my feet out of the net. Turn Yourself to me, and have mercy on me, For I am desolate and afflicted. The*

troubles of my heart have enlarged; Bring me out of my distresses! Look on my affliction and my pain, And forgive all my sins. Consider my enemies, for they are many; And they hate me with cruel hatred. Keep my soul, and deliver me; Let me not be ashamed, for I put my trust in You. Let integrity and uprightness preserve me, For I wait for You. Redeem Israel, O God, out of all their troubles!

This life is a crazy adventure, and what the Lord wants to reveal to us about Himself, including His love for us, will amaze us! Let us give Him that opportunity to show us who He is, and what He wants to impart to us. Let us give Him the opportunity to transform us into the image of Jesus. Let us give Him the opportunity to shower His peace and joy on us, giving us the opportunity to receive it and live it. We have to fight through the difficulties of life. Trials will come. They will keep coming. But we have the Lord. We have an inheritance. We can fight in His goodness and blessing. And, we can fight the good fight!

So fight on!

Made in the USA
Monee, IL
23 June 2020